a countercultural life

living well in a broken world

by STUART BRISCOE

A book from Stuart Briscoe and *Telling the Truth*

ISBN: 978-1-934590-92-8

First published in the United States of America

Cover and interior design by Hope Certalic

a countercultural life

living well in a broken world

by STUART BRISCOE

Introduction

You and I live in a mixed-up world that embraces numerous worldviews that differ widely from a Christian worldview.

Now, I know that this is a statement of the obvious, but I believe we often struggle as followers of Jesus Christ to figure out ***how*** to live in such a world. It is fallen and broken, driven by values and views that run counter to our faith and to the truth of Scripture—and we wonder how best to relate.

Should we isolate ourselves from such a world, trying to keep ourselves "unstained"? Should we be intimidated by what our secular counterparts believe because we feel "out of step"? Then again, maybe we should identify more closely with the values of our world in order to win more people to Christ.

While I am confident we can name Christians who relate to our world in each of these ways, there is one other option I believe we should explore. One other option that I believe is the proper biblical choice for each of us as Christ's followers.

Over the next several pages, it is my intention to guide you on this journey to discover how to live in a broken world as a Christ follower, and I want to do so by looking at the life of Joseph (Genesis 37-50). What I believe we will find is an excellent model for how we should indeed live in our world.

The Life of Joseph:
God's plan for his life *and* ours

By the time Joseph was thirty, he had packed more into his three decades than most people experience in two or three lifetimes. Beginning in Genesis 37, when he was just seventeen he was betrayed by his brothers and sold into Egyptian slavery. He became the property of a man called Potiphar who quickly discovered that he had bought an exceptional teenager.

Joseph, against all odds, succeeded in conducting himself wisely and well in ways that belied his youth. Bereft of his freedom and any viable options, Joseph applied himself to living well where he was—in slavery. It's hard to say, and harder to believe, but he was an astounding success as a slave!

Once his true value was recognized, he was promoted to a trusted and significant position in Potiphar's household. There he did extremely well until Potiphar's wife falsely accused him of trying to rape her. In fact, she had tried to seduce him, and he refused her.

William Congreve, the 17th century British dramatist writing millennia later than the author of Genesis, explained, *"Hell hath no fury, like a woman scorned!"* Joseph discovered this very early in life. Potiphar believed his wife's story, rejected Joseph's explanation, and the young man was thrown into prison.

Joseph soon established himself as a model prisoner and an invaluable aid to the prison warden, until eventually he was effectively running the prison. He even made a success of incarceration!

While he was in prison, two officials from Pharaoh's court were thrown into jail, charged with the heinous crime of upsetting Pharaoh. They were held at Pharaoh's pleasure, and during this time both men had dreams.

Now, in ancient times it was not uncommon for people to invest their dreams with deep spiritual significance and to put great weight on their interpretation. So Joseph was called upon to interpret the dreams of each of these men, which he did.

> "God had not overlooked him. Joseph was remembered in the courts of heaven."

Interpreting one of the men's dream, Joseph predicted the man would be immediately restored to his position of authority, which he was. However, Joseph predicted that the other man would be hanged, which also occurred.

Naturally, the former was delighted, and the only thing Joseph asked of him was, "Please don't forget me; put in a good word for me to Pharaoh." Unfortunately, once the man was released from jail, he failed on both counts and for two more years, Joseph languished in prison—abused, victimized, falsely accused, banished to the trash can of the public's recollections!

There is an underlying theme in the story of Joseph that we should not miss. While we focus on the pathos of the inhuman, unjust victimization of this young man and the cruel disappointments that relentlessly came his way, God had not overlooked him. Joseph was remembered in the courts of heaven. Twice in Genesis 39 we are told *"the LORD was with Joseph"* and that Joseph succeeded because *"the LORD gave him success."*

As the story unfolds, we begin to realize that Joseph's success was not a matter of luck, fate, or coincidence—this young man was part of a divine plan so vast that it would never be accomplished in his lifetime or, in fact, for generations.

Surprisingly—this is true for us all.

Growing up, Joseph's older brothers called him "The Dreamer" with good reason. Even as a teenager he had not only shown a tendency to dream but also a gift for the interpretation of dreams. Occasionally this ability got him into trouble. In a couple of dreams that Joseph interpreted for his brothers, he told them in effect, "The day will come, when you, my older brothers, will bow down to me." Then he went to his father and told him basically the same thing.

Neither father nor brothers were receptive to this information. But Joseph had it right because God had revealed this information to him. Even at that stage of young Joseph's life, God was working out His plan, and the day was going to come when they actually *would* bow down to him! This is how it happened!

Follow God's lead and watch what He can do through you

While Joseph was still incarcerated, Pharaoh had some dreams, and he called in his professional interpreters and his magicians, who ended up being no help at all! The dreams were very basic and very simple. He dreamt that there were seven very fat, healthy-looking cows and seven very meager, emaciated cows, and the skinny ones ate up the fat cows. Then to reinforce the message and give it a note of urgency, he had another dream where there were seven very fruitful sheaves of corn, and seven very skinny, blighted ones, and the blighted ones ate up the mature ones.

These dreams were very troubling to Pharaoh, but he couldn't find anyone who could interpret them for him. Then the former prisoner, who had forgotten Joseph, suddenly remembered him and said to Pharaoh, "I remember my shortcomings!" (That's always a good thing to do.) "There's a young Hebrew down in the prison who could interpret your dreams for you."

So Joseph was summoned and ushered into Pharaoh's presence. He listened as the mighty ruler recounted the dreams. But when Pharaoh asked for an interpretation, Joseph instead gave a disclaimer. He said, "I can't, but God will show you."

I can't, but God can

There, incidentally, is one of the keys to Joseph. He knew what he couldn't do, but he knew what God *could* do with somebody who knows what God can do! Joseph's theme all along had been and continued to be, "I can't, but God can." That's worth repeating—"I can't, but God can!"

So Joseph interpreted the dream and told Pharaoh, "Pharaoh, you are going to have seven years of bumper crops followed by seven years of devastating famine. Now, this is the thing to do—during the seven bumper years, let's be prudent. Let's take one-fifth of all the bumper crops and store them under your control."

Pharaoh immediately saw the possibilities of this arrangement and listened intently as Joseph added, "But you need somebody who has the know-how to put all this together!" Pharaoh looked at Joseph and he said, *"Can we find anyone like this man, one in whom is the spirit of God?"* (Genesis 41:38).

Isn't that interesting? Pharaoh could have said, "Here's a smart businessman, he's got keen insights into economics, and he seems to have a happy knack of foreseeing the future. Knowledge is power and anyone with a visionary knowledge of the future is worth his weight in gold. I could use him to solidify my position in the nation and around the whole area." All this would have been true, but Pharaoh, even though he was no good at interpreting dreams, did know a spiritual man if and when he encountered one. And he had one right in front of him. A spiritual man!

Not only did Pharaoh recognize a spiritual man, he appreciated him! He liked what he saw. He recognized the "value" of the man! He wanted to honor him and respect him, and, no doubt, to benefit from him, too!

> "A spiritual man—living in a situation that was far from ideal in every sense—radiated goodness, significance, value, and integrity, and Pharaoh knew it."

This remarkable evaluation of Joseph was made by a powerful king whose values, beliefs, and lifestyles were far removed from those of the young man interpreting his dreams. And Joseph's world—cruel, unjust, vindictive, exploitative—was very different from Pharaoh's cosseted, silver-spoon-in-his-mouth existence where his every whim became a command and every displeasure merited a prison sentence. Yet Pharaoh, who had so much at his disposal and so much to offer, was beholden to Joseph who had nothing but his integrity, and yet so much to share that the king recognized and respected.

The life of Joseph. A spiritual man—living in a situation that was far from ideal in every sense—radiated goodness, significance, value, and integrity, and Pharaoh knew it. A spiritual man!

Successful, spiritual people

The situations in which we live are far removed from those of Joseph the falsely accused, exiled prisoner-slave. Our circumstances may be considerably less appealing than we would like them to be, but they don't compare with those of Joseph, whom God enabled to succeed regardless of his circumstances. We too are called to be a success as spiritual people. And Joseph can be our long-departed guide to remind us of his double secret—God was ***with*** him and ***God*** gave him success.

Jesus used different terminology when addressing this topic. He talked about His disciples—and us—being "the salt of the earth" and "the light of the world." And through His teaching to them, He reminded us that if the light was hidden under a bushel, or the salt lost its saltiness, neither would be any good!

When talking about the light of the world, Jesus was, effectively, telling His followers, "I am placing you intentionally in a dark world in order for you to bring light to bear on the gloom and to give points of reference to those stumbling in darkness!" Or looking at the "salty" analogy He used, we can infer that He was saying to us, "There is a lot of tasteless stuff going on in society; corruption rules. But salt adds flavor and arrests corruption. What we need is a dash of salt—and that is where you come in—you are the salt!"

That's part of the reason Joseph was where he was and we are where we are. Joseph in Pharaoh's court; we in our everyday circles of influence. Spiritual men, spiritual women, in society—our environment—to bring light into spiritual darkness and salt into a world decaying in sin.

> "spiritual men, spiritual women, bring light into spiritual darkness and salt into a world decaying in sin."

So Joseph was given his place of authority, and he managed the monumental crisis with great success. But it is doubtful that he would have imagined in his wildest dreams the scenario that was about to unfold. Because, far away from the palace in Egypt where Joseph now moved in the corridors of power, his father and his brothers were facing famine-induced starvation. They'd heard there was food in Egypt, so, in desperation, they headed south.

Eventually they arrived in Pharaoh's court where they appeared before the person presiding over the distribution of the food. Such was his obvious position of authority—and they were so utterly destitute and desperate—that they prostrated themselves before the unrecognized—and unrecognizable—Joseph. What Joseph had predicted years previously was coming true, but the story is running ahead of itself!

Real spirituality

Let's think about what it means to be a spiritual person. First of all, let's be clear what we mean by "a spiritual person."

For a time, the words "spiritual" or "spirituality" were superfluous in our materialistic world. Science ruled, technology triumphed, faith was obsolete. The material world was real and everything else was myth. If you couldn't touch it, taste it, see it, or measure it, it was neither true nor real… and certainly not important. God was either dead, seriously ill, had lost interest, mislaid His manual, or had retired. By any standard of reckoning, He was irrelevant.

But more recently, attitudes changed. In our scientifically driven, technologically savvy world, we humans had grown accustomed to assuming that answers to our problems would be found in our inventions, and that mankind held the keys to Utopia or Shangri-La or whatever else was envisaged by futurists and promised by politicians. But despite all the remarkable scientific advances and all the technological benefits, people still complained of a lack of meaning, purpose, significance, and fulfillment in their lives.

In other words, material answers undoubtedly provided an abundance of material advantages, amenities, and luxuries, and for many people, their standards of living rose dramatically (although sadly many were still left far behind). However, even the most privileged recognized an inner lack of something, feelings of dissatisfaction and disappointment with life. Repeatedly they complained, "Things are not the way they ought to be." Thoughtful, honest people began to accept that materialism—confidence in material things to provide all that mankind needs to experience all that mankind desires to have and be—had failed to meet the deepest longings of the human heart. It required no great leap of insight to recognize that after all, perhaps there was another dimension to our humanity. And if it wasn't material, it must be spiritual. A new spirituality was in the process of being born.

> "Materialism had failed to meet the deepest longings of the human heart."

Don't be confused about this! The new "spirituality" was born out of a spiritual hunger that would not go away ***and*** disappointment that the measurable domains of science, technology, and material things had failed to satisfy the insatiable human appetite for reality. But like a young person caught on the rebound from a failed romance, humanity lurched unthinkingly and unwisely into the welcoming arms of worldviews and lifestyles based on free experimentation and the embracing of otherworldly pursuits. Spirituality became an "umbrella term" to describe just about anything that imaginative, lively people could conjure up—provided it was not material.

This trendy spirituality was ardently promoted by the entertainment industry. We see it exemplified in vampires and ghosts, and angels and demons who were let loose. In addition, after-death experiences, mystical encounters, and paranormal phenomena proliferated and held people spellbound. Eastern mysticism—the more exotic the better—was embraced, and gurus were in great demand. Spirituality had been redefined and refurbished, and the new "spiritual people" came to the fore.

None of this should be confused with the kind of spirituality we are talking about! Bill Hybels, the senior pastor of Willow Creek Community Church, says, "In America today, there is a great interest in 'spirituality' just so long as it doesn't involve truth." He's right, and I would add, the "truth," for instance, of a God who is sovereign! The "truth" that we are sinners who stand condemned before a holy God! The "truth" that we cannot save ourselves! The "truth" that only Christ can save! The "truth" that in the death and the resurrection of Christ and the acknowledgment of His saving Lordship, we begin to discover what it means to be reconciled to God and indwelt by His Spirit.

Let the Holy Spirit move in your fallenness and regenerate you

There is great interest in spirituality, just so long as it doesn't involve dealing with sin, leading to repentance, and acknowledging the Lordship of Christ. When this happens, it alerts me to a biblical understanding of spirituality that has its roots in an experience of the Holy Spirit. Those of us who place our trust in Jesus Christ, the Bible tells us, are indwelt by the very Spirit of God that Jesus promised in John 16.

And therein lies the key! *The spiritual person we're talking about is the person who has a living relationship with the Holy Spirit*—or to use Pharaoh's terminology, "a man (or woman) in whom is the Spirit of God."

Paul underlined this when writing to the troublesome Corinthian church, *"Brothers and sisters, I could not address you as people who live by the Spirit but as people who are still worldly—mere infants in Christ."* But immediately added, *"Don't you know that you yourselves are God's temple and that God's Spirit dwells in your midst?"* (1 Corinthians 3:1,16). Paul was alarmed that the Corinthians apparently either did not know or did not care to know about the Holy Spirit and His indwelling.

This reminds me of the story of a couple sitting in church. The pastor announced the topic of his sermon: "Today I want to talk to you about ignorance and apathy."

"What's ignorance and apathy?" asked the young woman.

"I don't know and I don't care," replied the young man, displaying his disinterest in the proceedings and unwittingly more wisdom than he knew he possessed! He would have been at home in First Church of Corinth!

This is not a subject for apathy or ignorance, as it is the great mystery that Paul alludes to in Colossians 1:26-27… the mystery that has been hidden since the dawn of time, "Christ in you, the hope of glory." The indwelling Christ. The fact that we would have His Spirit placed within us was a secret God had kept for eons. And it is this power that is the key to living in a world like ours.

When thinking about the Holy Spirit, I like to remember a certain easily demonstrable truth concerning Him. *Whenever God does anything big His Spirit is involved.*

In Genesis 1:2 we encounter the first reference to God's Spirit. There we are told, "*In the beginning God created the heavens and the earth. Now the earth was formless and empty, darkness was over the surface of the deep, and the Spirit of God was hovering over the waters.*" What was happening? In the formative stages of God's work of bringing the created order into being, there was apparently a stage, an era, a time (what terminology can we use to speak of something as dramatic and beyond our comprehension as the creative activity of the Divine Originator?) when formlessness gave way to order. This was the work of the Spirit. He was active in ***creation.***

A breath of fresh air

The Hebrew word for "Spirit" *(Ruach)* also means "wind" or "breath." So it might help us to understand this Scripture by imagining a powerful wind, a life-giving breath of fresh air moving into and over formlessness and creatively bringing order out of chaos. A benevolent Hurricane Katrina, a creative Superstorm Sandy. This was the work of God's Spirit… the very same Spirit of God that got under young Joseph's skin—and it showed!

Man fell from grace, became estranged from God, alienation set into the individual heart, fragmentation in societal relationship—the fallen world that we encounter wherever we look today was born. But God, grieved at what had transpired in His beautiful world, did not destroy it, discount it, or desert it. He set about redeeming it. Immediately He began to speak His mind, to reveal His plans, to proclaim His Word to people to remind them of who He was and what He was going to do! But how? He set His Spirit to work in the lives of His prophets who then spoke! Peter stated bluntly, *"Prophets, though human, spoke from God as they were carried along by the Holy Spirit"* (2 Peter 1:21). The prophets pointed out unerringly that God's purposes would come to fulfillment in His Messiah! This became the great hope of Israel. And it was generated by the mighty work of the Spirit. He was busy in ***proclamation.***

One day Messiah came—but not as expected. We are told that He was born of a virgin, and that which was born in her was born of the Holy Spirit (Luke 1:26-38). The Spirit was involved in the ***incarnation.***

Jesus lived in obscurity for thirty years and then He burst on the scene at His baptism. The Holy Spirit came upon Him, and in the fullness of the Spirit, He was led into the wilderness where He confronted the evil one, whom He comprehensively defeated. The Spirit aided Him in countering ***temptation*** (Luke 4:1-14).

"His job is to woo us and draw us to Christ and to accomplish in us the miracle of the new birth."

Jesus moved to Jerusalem where the opposition grew, the hostility increased, and where treachery, betrayal, false charges, unjust sentence, scourging, and finally crucifixion were His lot. On the cross, where He experienced ignominy, shame, agony, alienation, and separation from God, He cried from the depths of His soul, *"My God, my God, why have you forsaken me?"* (Psalm 22:1; Mark 15:34). To think that the Eternal Son, ever with the Father, was now deserted is unspeakably heart wrenching, and in awe we ask, "How could He possibly go through all this?" Scripture tells us! It was *"through the eternal Spirit (that He) offered himself unblemished to God"* (Hebrews 9:14). The Spirit was empowering Him in ***crucifixion.***

But He didn't stay dead; on the third day He rose again from the dead. The greatest event in human history. The divine seal of approval on Christ's work of sacrificial atonement. The triumph of God over evil, the defeating of death, and the basis of hope everlasting. And guess what! Scripture says, *"If the Spirit of him who raised Jesus from the dead is living in you, he who raised Christ from the dead will also give life to your mortal bodies because of his Spirit who lives in you"* (Romans 8:11). The Spirit was powerfully in action in the ***resurrection***!

And note carefully, our ultimate resurrection is directly linked to the resurrection of Jesus and the work of the Spirit.

The Bible also tells us that it is the work of the Holy Spirit to move in the darkness of our fallenness—to open our eyes to the truth of our own condition and to reveal to us the reality and the beauty of Christ. His job is to woo us and draw us to Christ and to accomplish in us the miracle of the new birth. Remember that Jesus said, much to the surprise of His distinguished visitor, Nicodemus, that unless he was *"born of the Spirit"* (John 3:1-8), he would neither see nor enter God's Kingdom! The principle applies to all of us. So the Spirit is crucially at work in ***regeneration.***

There's one more thing to bear in mind.

In the same way that when a baby is born, a new life is only beginning, so also a person who is "born of the Spirit" is beginning a new life. And as life produces growth, whether in babies or in trees, so spiritual growth is to be expected where God's Spirit is present. This takes the form of a transforming work in attitudes, desires, aspirations, longings, character, behavior, and lifestyle. It's not instantaneous. And it's not always pleasant. It involves repenting, rethinking, revising, renewing, resolving, reorienting. The apostle Paul described it as follows: *"And we all, who with unveiled faces contemplate the Lord's glory, are being transformed into his image with ever-increasing glory, which comes from the Lord, who is the Spirit"* (2 Corinthians 3:18). The Spirit specializes in ***transformation.***

So as we think about the work of God's Spirit, we see that He is active from beginning to end in God's plan, in…

- Creation
- Proclamation
- Incarnation
- Temptation
- Crucifixion
- Resurrection
- Regeneration
- Transformation

Whenever God does anything big, He does it by His Spirit!

This was the Spirit who was operating in Joseph's life and was recognizable to Pharaoh. It is He who indwells the modern believer and who wishes to be clearly in evidence to the world in which that believer lives and moves and has her being.

So what is spirituality? Spirituality is the work of God's Spirit in the human spirit. It is a resultant lifestyle that exposes the transforming work of the Spirit to such an extent that slowly but surely Christ's likeness is reflected—and recognized. And regularly, but not, I'm afraid, always appreciated!

Live by the Spirit and use your spiritual gifts to serve God and others

That brings me back to Joseph standing before Pharaoh as he identified something of God's Spirit in the young man.

As Pharaoh watched this young man, Joseph, in action, he concluded that the young man, in some way, enjoyed a relationship with "God's Spirit." It may be that Pharaoh was so enamored with Joseph's gift of accurate interpretation of dreams that he needed nothing more to convince him of the Spirit's presence and activity in Joseph's life. And, of course, there is little doubt that we read more into Pharaoh's words than he himself understood. Provided we don't read into Scripture more than Scripture teaches, this is not only legitimate, it's necessary.

> "He concluded that the young man enjoyed a relationship with God's Spirit."

Compared to the privileged position we enjoy as New Testament era believers, the king was limited in his understanding of God's work in Joseph's life, in particular, and in human experience, in general. In fact, the Spirit has revealed many things to us in our day, even more than was revealed to Jesus' disciples while He was present with them. Jesus recognized this and alerted His disciples to the deficiencies in their understanding and of the necessity for the Spirit's ongoing work. *"I have much more to say to you, more than you can now bear. But when he, the Spirit of truth, comes, he will guide you into all the truth"* (John 16:12-13). So, our understanding of the Spirit's life and work is far superior to that of Pharaoh.

> "Can we find a man or woman or a boy or girl quite like this person here, who has had such a vital experience of Jesus as savior that the mighty spirit of the living God has chosen to make their body His holy temple and it is obvious?"

Pharaoh's question—whether it was rhetorical or not—would sound something like this if it were transported to the 21st century: "Can we find a man or woman or a boy or girl quite like this person here, who has had such a vital experience of Jesus as Savior that the mighty Spirit of the living God has chosen to make their body His holy temple and it is obvious?"

Bearing much fruit

While spirituality has its hidden roots in an experience of the Holy Spirit, its definitive fruits are clearly in evidence in various expressions of the Spirit. This is expressed in what Paul called "the fruit of the Spirit," which he further listed as *"love, joy, peace, forbearance, kindness, goodness, faithfulness, gentleness and self-control"* (Galatians 5:22-23).

For example, it is relatively easy for us to read the story of Joseph's "roller-coaster" life and to recognize in it, to an extraordinary degree, the love, and joy, and peace, and forbearance, and kindness, and gentleness, and self-control in his lifestyle that can be attributed to the work of the Spirit. He'd experienced enough to drive him crazy! He had gone through enough to make him the most bitter, vindictive person on the face of God's green earth! Amazingly, he didn't demonstrate these characteristics.

I have a suggestion for you that I believe will prove quite instructive. Read through the story of Joseph in Genesis chapters 39 to 48 inclusive, then add Genesis 49:22-26 as a postscript from his father. As you read, take note of the way in which, as he passed from one challenge to another, each challenge became the arena in which yet another aspect of the fruit of the Spirit was produced in his life. Sometimes love was called for. For example, when the brothers who had left him for dead appeared on his doorstep absolutely at his mercy. Other times patience in abundance was evident. Years and years in prison for a crime you did not commit requires more than human patience! Self-control was a daily requirement, not only as he faced the alluring Mrs. Potiphar, but also in later years, as he was showered with the excesses of Pharaoh's court. The differing aspects of the fruit of the Spirit were all there at one time or another. A spiritual man indeed!

In our daily lives it should not be difficult for us to see how easily we are swayed and molded by the thinking and behaving of the modern world. But frequently we do not see it, or if we do see it, we dismiss it as insignificant. We are like people living in a smog-ridden city, breathing in foul air constantly and adapting to it so thoroughly that we become inured to it, oblivious of it, and infected by it. We can become so much a creature of our times and our culture that we lose the distinctives that in other situations might call from our neighbors the unsolicited testimonial—"Can we find such a girl as this, a girl in whom the Spirit of God lives? Look at the love, joy, patience!"

That state of affairs can be remedied by the simple, disciplined application of life in the Spirit one step at a time. One situation after another. A life of awareness of His presence, recognition of His working, obedience to His promptings, and dependence upon His enabling.

Gifts for the common good

"However, the expression of the Holy Spirit in a spiritual person is not only seen in the Spirit's fruit, but also in the exercise of the gifts He imparts!"

Paul taught the Corinthian believers, *"Now about the gifts of the Spirit, brothers and sisters, I do not want you to be uninformed."* Then after explaining that the gifts themselves vary because the tasks in which they are to be employed vary, he added, *"All these are the work of one and the same Spirit, and he distributes them to each one, just as he determines"* (1 Corinthians 12:11). In other words, all who are indwelt by the Holy Spirit—that is, all true believers in Jesus—receive from the Holy Spirit the unique ability-imparting spiritual gifts necessary for them to engage in acts of service that are an appropriate response to God's goodness (which is the essence of worship). Paul said these acts of service were "for the common good," by which he apparently meant the well-being of the community of faith to which the new believer belongs, as well as the broader community where the need for ministries of mercy and grace is desperately obvious.

An attitude of sacrificial service does not come naturally to us humans, and it is to be admitted that Spirit-imparted gifts can lie dormant, gathering dust, unless the recipients also know something of Spirit-imparted motivation. This comes first from the example of Jesus, who said, *"The Son of Man did not come to be served, but to serve"* (Matthew 20:28), which the Spirit-endued believer gradually embraces. When that happens, attitudes are changed and acts of glad service become normative.

So informed and moved, stimulated and motivated, the spiritual person reaches out, seeking to bless rather than be blessed—in the power of the Spirit, in the unique and distinctive enabling of the Spirit's power and gifts.

There's another thing we can learn from the story of Joseph. Pharaoh asked him, "Can you interpret my dreams?" And the young Hebrew replied, "No, I can't, but God can!"

The person who understands "giftedness" knows perfectly well that anything that he or she achieves is directly related to the fact that it is God who graciously gave the gift, as well as the desire and the power, and therefore the glory belongs to Him! This means that it should not be hard to identify a spiritual person in a materialistic environment.

A petunia in an onion patch

We used to sing a little song in England when I was a kid. I can only remember one line of the lyrics: *"I'm as lonely as a petunia in an onion patch!"* I had no idea then—or now!—what a petunia looks like, but I got the drift. It was something markedly different and readily distinguishable from an onion! And if it bloomed in the midst of a crop of onions, it was unlikely it would be overlooked!

Maybe the idea of being a spiritual person in a materialistic world doesn't grab you. How about thinking of yourself being planted, like a petunia, in the middle of onions? Is that more appealing? You look around and you say, "Well, I guess I am a little different. The people walking past no doubt have noticed me."

Then, as a spiritual person, look at your family, or the place where you work, or the college where you are studying, or the ball team that you play on, and ask yourself a petunia question—"Why in the world am I here?" The answer presumably is, "Because you were planted there in that environment in order that you might live as a spiritual person, and express your spirituality in fruits and in the exercise of gifts!"

This is what Joseph set out to do wherever he found himself. Like the petunia, he was frequently lonesome, but, also, like the fragrant bloom, his very presence changed his environment for the good.

Speak the truth

But there's another thing we should notice about Joseph. He spoke the truth. It may be possible to criticize him for speaking imprudently—even though it was truthful—to his brothers about their eventual subservience to him. And no doubt he managed to offend his father when he informed him of a similar outcome. Youthful exuberance, inexperience, and brashness perhaps? But it all happened to be true.

We observe this same trait in prison as he interpreted the dreams of Pharaoh's officials. He did not back off from telling one of them that his days were numbered. No doubt, that didn't help his popularity rating, particularly when he told the other man he would be free in short order. But it was the truth. And when he explained about the impending seven years of plenty followed by seven years of famine, he did not yield to the temptation to stress the positive and soft-pedal the negative.

He also spoke the truth about the God factor to people who did not share his Hebraic worldview. When speaking of God, there was no mention from Joseph of Geb, Nut and Shu, Ra and Isis, although these gods were deeply revered by the Egyptians. He represented the God of his fathers, the God of Abraham, Isaac, and Jacob who had revealed Himself and His purposes throughout the history of the Hebrew people. In marked contrast to the popular polytheistic lore of Egypt, Joseph unabashedly represented the One true God, and he spoke truthfully about Him.

The Egyptians recognized the uncomfortable fact that their very survival was directly related to the vagaries of the weather and, in particular, the cycles of the great River Nile. But they believed all these factors were governed by the capricious pantheon of gods. And their religious observances were designed to placate these unpredictable "deities" and to curry favor with them if at all possible. In contrast, Joseph stood tall and told Pharaoh, in reference to the dream and its interpretation and application to the well-being of his nation, *"The matter has been firmly decided by God, and God will do it soon"* (Genesis 41:32). Not exactly politically correct in Pharaoh's court! But true!

A modern day spiritual person will be equally convinced that God is in charge and will demonstrate that he or she is pleased about it, and will not be at all reluctant to say so!

T.S. Eliot wrote, "Humankind cannot bear very much reality." Reality is another word for truth. So anyone committed to truth-telling must be ready, like Joseph, to have his words fall on deaf ears or to be thrown back in his face. Undeterred, he continues to anoint the hearer's ears with the reality of truth, rather than tickle them with soothing platitudes that mislead and half-truths that conceal. Truth spoken with grace, presented in lockstep with concern, and backed up by credibility will seek out hearts that long for words that hold the ring of truth. There truth will find a home, and the hearers will find the help and hope and healing they long for. Every time this happens a miracle is a distinct possibility. Onions morph into petunias! This is what we are called to, and that is why we are here.

Know the truth and demonstrate Christ to your world

Our focus has been on the petunia. Now, for a brief period, let's look at the onion patch in light of the days in which we are living. A brief comparison of the prevailing contemporary materialistic mind-set (infiltrated by the presence of the new age spirituality) and a spiritual belief system and lifestyle may help.

The materialist mind-set says,

- "Man is the center of the universe, not God."
- "Time is the extent of experience, not eternity."
- "Earth is the limit of our environment, not the heavens."
- "Visible, tangible, measurable matter is the measure of value, not spiritual and invisible realities!"

The GPS (global positioning system) found in many high-end cars is extremely valuable. It not only shows a driver the exact position of the vehicle, but if it is correctly programmed, it will outline, in addition to position, the desired destination and the best route to get there. It will often include a voice, either male or female (American or British), that will articulate instructions and proffer rebukes if they are ignored. The key, of course, is to ensure that the data programmed into the system is accurate, or the destination will be incorrect, the route will be misleading, and the driver will be lost.

So it is with mind-sets and belief systems. Correct information programmed into the human heart puts you on the right path and gets you to the right destination. Just take another look at the differences between the spiritual and the secular mind-set, and you will see how easily the routes taken through life differ, and, of course, the eternal destinations will eventually differ more than can be envisioned.

The challenge for Joseph, or any spiritually-minded person—the petunia—is how to relate to the place they are planted. There are at least four different ways, all of which are quite common—identification, intimidation, isolation, and infiltration.

Identification. Joseph clearly identified with Egypt in that he was born there, lived there, ate their food, and breathed their air. In addition, he obviously had many things in common with the Egyptians… even to the extent of sharing a cell with other unfortunates.

The same could be said about me. I have lived more than half my life among the people of Wisconsin, and clearly I identify with them at many levels most heartily and thankfully. But they are known for their "brats" and their cheese washed down with copious drafts of Old Milwaukee while "tailgating" in the freezing cold of parking lots before Green Bay Packers games. And for some inexplicable reason, they wear "cheeseheads." Now, I happen to believe that brats and cheese and Old Milwaukee can be, and often are, injurious to one's health and well-being—so I avoid them! I also believe that cheeseheads are injurious to a person's image! Moreover, I think the warmth and comfort of my home are much more congenial to longevity than freezing parking lots.

Perhaps most significantly, over fifty-five years ago—before I ever heard of the Green Bay Packers' existence—I became a "dyed-in-the-wool" (red and white) fan of the English soccer team Manchester United, rather than the green and gold of the Packers! So I identify—but up to a limit! Now I'll admit that, as a result of these limits of my identification, some of my neighbors tend to classify me in much the same way as they'd characterize a solitary onion in a petunia bed. But the reality is this—there are limits because total identification results in lack of distinction.

I've spoken, by way of analogy, of the negative aspects of standing out in a crowd. By what I don't do. But is it all about negativity? No. The positive side of being distinctive is that it gives me a platform so that when I speak up it is going to be beneficial—as in the case of Joseph and the famine. He began to talk like no one else around him. His message not only had the ring of truth, it was arresting, hopeful, practical, and compelling, and led to even Pharaoh being galvanized into action that spelled "survival" for millions in the Middle East. Joseph was different. He spoke differently because he had a different allegiance as he lived among those who differed from him. And he did it in such a way that the identification he had developed with the Egyptians gave him access to them at the point of their differentiation.

Surely the best example of this is that of our Lord. For instance, He identified with the woman he met at Sychar's well (read the story in John 4). He did not meet her at the point of her lifestyle, which was scandalous, but at the point of her need, which He fully understood and was more than ready to address. This is the balance we need to maintain.

Intimidation. To be hauled out of a prison cell straight into the palatial surroundings of the Egyptian court would be intimidating enough! But Joseph knew from the experience of the courtiers he had met in prison that getting things wrong in Pharaoh's presence, or giving a dream interpretation that the Pharaoh did not want to hear, could be a capital offense! He could pay with his life. So he could have been intimidated.

My elder son was a boy of few words, and grew up to be a man of few words! Before praying with him one evening, I said, "Do the kids at school ever give you a hard time?"

"No."

"Do they embarrass you before the other kids? Do they tease you about being a preacher's kid? A Christian?"

"NO!"

"Do you want to pray about it?"

"No need!"

"No need to pray?" I asked.

"No need to pray about this," he replied.

"Don't they give you a hard time because you are a Christian?" I inquired, remembering my own school experience.

"NO!"

I said, "Well, when I was a kid in school and said anything about being a Christian, they gave me a hard time!"

"That's not my problem!" my son said confidently.

"Well, Dave, if you tell them you're a Christian, they will give you a hard time!"

He looked up and showed some interest for the first time, and he said, "Better not tell them then!"

How do you like the logic of kids? It's very simple. If they give you a hard time because you're a Christian, keep your mouth shut! That's the language of intimidation, and that's exactly where a lot of folks are today! But not Joseph!

Isolation. There are certainly risks attached to living voluntarily or involuntarily in a challenging environment. Like Egypt, for instance. Joseph had been in places where he could have been killed, where he was sold, where he might have been seduced, where he was imprisoned, where he could have offended the king—he'd lived in one precarious situation after another all his young life. And this, no doubt, can make the bravest soul a little nervous.

On an entirely different level, there are situations in which the believer lives in this fallen world that make us nervous, too. And, understandably, we take precautions and avoid them if at all possible. This is true not only in terms of physical danger but also of spiritual reefs and shoals on which we can be shipwrecked.

Identifying with an unbelieving community, spending time, engaging in interests, developing friendships can all be taken to an extent that does more harm than good. And some people, aware of this, decide that isolation is the only safe response. It's similar to the argument for a teetotal approach to drinking wine. Scripture forbids drunkenness for it leads to irresponsible, unrestrained behavior that is not becoming of a disciple of Jesus (see Ephesians 5:18). But it also teaches the legitimacy of and the medicinal advantages of taking a "little wine" (see 1 Timothy 3:8, 5:23).

A teetotal approach to wine drinking is prudent, wise, careful, and is a sure safeguard against drunkenness. If you never touch it, you'll never get drunk from it! That's a no-brainer. So far so good. But is it biblical? I'll leave you to decide. But as far as our study is concerned, the question is, "Given the risks inherent in involvement in relations with unbelievers is isolation from them wise, prudent, careful, and a sure safeguard against spiritual downfall?" If you have nothing to do with them, they can't influence you! That's another no-brainer. But is it biblical?

No, it isn't. Isolation is not an option.

Infiltration. When I was the senior pastor of Elmbrook Church, I loved the way we ended our annual Christmas Eve services. As the lights in the large auditorium were dimmed to nearly dark, I took a single candle, lit it, and held it high… a small, insignificant glimmer in the darkness. Then one by one, others stepped forward and lit their candles from mine, then made their way into the congregation until two or three thousand candles were glowing. One by one, we demonstrated what Jesus had said, "You are the light of the world." The auditorium was transformed—the light had infiltrated the darkness and slowly but surely banished it.

So what is it to be? Identification, intimidation, isolation, or infiltration? I believe Joseph has the answer for us.

As "one in whom is the Spirit of God," he infiltrated his culture and his world with the fruit of the Spirit, expressing the truth and reality of His God. And the same is our call today. As "one in whom is the Spirit of God," you have God's Spirit in you. The Spirit who is at work to express His fruit and who has gifted you in your unique sphere of influence to demonstrate Christ to your world.

You are a petunia in an onion patch. Light in a dark world. Salt in a culture that is decaying each day. Like Joseph, go infiltrate your world in His power and for His glory!